# Remembrance of
## My First Holy Communion

Name __John__

Address __120 charls St,__

City __F.P,__

State __New york__


## I received Holy Communion


in _____the_____ Church

on _____last year March 21,94_____

# I Pray with Jesus

by
**The Daughters of St. Paul**

**illustrated by
Dick Smolinski**

**St. Paul Books & Media**

Imprimatur:
+ Bernard Carndinal Law
    December 10, 1990

Nihil Obstat:
Greer G. Gordon

ISBN 0-8198-3629-X  hardcover
ISBN 0-8198-3630-3  deluxe white
ISBN 0-8198-3631-1  deluxe black

Revised edition, 1991

Printed and published in the U.S.A.
by St. Paul Books & Media
50 St. Paul's Avenue, Boston, MA 02130

St. Paul Books & Media is the publishing house of the
Daughters of St. Paul, an international congregation of
women religious serving the Church with the
communications media.

    3  4  5  6  7  8  9     99  98  97  96  95  94

# Contents

## PRAYER BEFORE
## A CRUCIFIX

Look down upon me, good and gentle Jesus, while I kneel before you. I ask you to give me faith, hope and love, true sorrow for my sins, and the desire to please you more and more. I look with great love and sorrow at your five wounds. And I remember the words which David your prophet said of you, my Jesus: "They have pierced my hands and my feet; they have counted all my bones."

# MORNING PRAYERS

I am awake now, Jesus, and I give you my first greeting:

In the Name of the Father and of the Son and of the Holy Spirit. Amen.

## I ADORE YOU

I adore you, my God, and I love you with all my heart. I thank you for having created me, made me a Christian and kept me this night.

Today I want to be good.

I want to be all yours.

Keep me from sin, Jesus.

Bless my father and my mother and all my friends. Amen.

JESUS, LET ME SPEND THIS NEW DAY
WITH YOU AND YOUR MOTHER.

**Now with you, dear Jesus, I will say the prayer that you taught the apostles:**

## OUR FATHER

Our Father, who art in heaven, hallowed be thy name. Thy kingdom come. Thy will be done on earth as it is in heaven. Give us this day our daily bread, and forgive us our trespasses as we forgive those who trespass against us. And lead us not into temptation; but deliver us from evil. Amen.

HEAVENLY FATHER,
BLESS ME THIS DAY.

Jesus, your Mother also is beside me, and to her I repeat the greeting of the Angel Gabriel.

## HAIL MARY

Hail, Mary, full of grace! The Lord is with you. Blessed are you among women, and blessed is the fruit of your womb, Jesus. Holy Mary, Mother of God, pray for us sinners now and at the hour of our death. Amen.

## GLORY

Glory to the Father, and to the Son, and to the Holy Spirit: as it was in the beginning, is now, and will be for ever. Amen.

"Hail, Mary, full of grace!"

**Dear Jesus, I thank you for
giving me an angel who watches
over me and who guards me from
dangers.**

## ANGEL OF GOD

Angel of God, my guardian dear,
to whom God's love entrusts me
here; ever this day be at my side, to
light and guard, to rule and guide.
Amen.

**Jesus, hear my prayer for those
dear to me who have died and who
may be in purgatory:**

## ETERNAL REST

Eternal rest grant to them, O
Lord, and let perpetual light shine
upon them. May they rest in peace.
Amen.

MY GUARDIAN ANGEL,
STAY EVER AT MY SIDE.

**Now, dear Jesus, one more greeting to Mary, your mother and mine, and then I am ready to start my day:**

## HAIL HOLY QUEEN

Hail, holy Queen, Mother of mercy, our life, our sweetness, and our hope. To you we cry, poor banished children of Eve; to you we send up our sighs, mourning and weeping in this valley of tears. Turn then, most gracious advocate, your eyes of mercy toward us; and after this our exile, show to us the blessed fruit of your womb, Jesus. O clement, O loving, O sweet Virgin Mary.

HOLY MARY, WATCH OVER ME ALWAYS.

# ACTS OF FAITH, HOPE, LOVE AND CONTRITION

Jesus, I believe in you, I hope in you and I love you. I ask pardon for my sins. I want to say these beautiful prayers:

## ACT OF FAITH

My God, I firmly believe that you are one God in three divine Persons, Father, Son and Holy Spirit. I believe that your divine Son became man and died for our sins, and that he will come to judge the living and the dead. I believe these and all the truths which the holy Catholic Church teaches, because

you have revealed them, who can
neither deceive nor be deceived.

## ACT OF HOPE

My God, relying on your infinite
goodness and promises, I hope to
obtain pardon of my sins, the help
of your grace, and life everlasting,
through the merits of Jesus Christ,
my Lord and Redeemer.

## ACT OF LOVE

My God, I love you above all
things, with my whole heart and
soul, because you are all good and
worthy of all love. I love my neighbor as myself for the love of you. I
forgive all who have injured me,
and I ask pardon of all whom I have
injured.

## ACT OF CONTRITION

My God,
I am sorry for my sins with all
    my heart.
In choosing to do wrong
and failing to do good,
I have sinned against you
whom I should love above all
    things.
I firmly intend, with your help,
to do penance,
to sin no more,
and to avoid whatever leads me
    to sin.
Our Savior Jesus Christ
suffered and died for us.
In his name, my God, have
    mercy.

THANK YOU, JESUS,
FOR THIS GOOD DAY.

# NIGHT PRAYERS

**Jesus, I started my day with you and I want to close it with you. I want to thank you for your goodness to me and my dear ones this day.**

## I ADORE YOU

I adore you, my God, and I love you with all my heart. I thank you for having created me, made me a Christian and kept me this day. Thank you for helping me do good things today! (Remember some of these good things.) I may have done some bad things, too. I am sorry for those choices. I know you forgive me. Guard me while I sleep and deliver me from dangers. May your grace be always with me and with all my dear ones. Amen.

**Now that I have asked your pardon, dear Jesus, I will pray to your Mother also:**

My dear Mother Mary, keep me safe in your care. Guard my mind, my heart and my senses, that I may never fall into sin. Make my thoughts, desires, words and actions holy so that I may please you and your Jesus, my God, and live with you, forever in heaven.

# VISIT TO JESUS IN THE BLESSED SACRAMENT

Jesus, you are my dearest Friend. You said: "Let the children come to me." You want me to visit you in church where you are always present in the Blessed Sacrament.

Jesus, I believe in you, I hope in you, and I love you.

Jesus, I give my whole heart to you. Bless those who love me and bless everyone.

JESUS, YOU ARE MY BEST FRIEND!

"Bless us, O Lord,..."

# MEAL PRAYERS

## BLESSING BEFORE MEALS

Bless us, O Lord, and these your gifts, which we are about to receive from your bounty, through Christ our Lord. Amen.

**Eat everything that your mother has prepared, without being fussy. If you like some food very much, do not take as much as you would like, but take a little less and offer it up as a sacrifice to Jesus.**

## BLESSING AFTER MEALS

We give you thanks for all your benefits, Almighty God, who live and reign forever; and may the souls of the faithful departed, through the mercy of God, rest in peace. Amen.

# THE EUCHARISTIC CELEBRATION (MASS)

The Mass is the sacrifice of Jesus Christ. The Mass is also called the Eucharistic Celebration.

In the Mass Jesus teaches you. Through the readings he tells you how to live as he lived.

Listen to the readings with all the people of God.

In the Mass Jesus offers himself to the heavenly Father, to make up for the sins of everyone.

Offer yourself with Jesus to our heavenly Father.

In the Mass Jesus makes himself your food. He will always be close to you as you walk toward heaven.

**Prepare yourself to receive Jesus into your heart in Holy Communion.**

# INTRODUCTORY RITE

**WE STAND.**

PRIEST:

In the name of the Father, and of the Son, and of the Holy Spirit.

PEOPLE: Amen.

PRIEST:

...to prepare ourselves to celebrate the sacred mysteries,

let us call to mind our sins.

PEOPLE:

I confess to almighty God, and to you, my brothers and sisters,

that I have sinned through my own fault

in my thoughts and in my words,

in what I have done,

and in what I have failed to do;
and I ask blessed Mary, ever
  virgin,
all the angels and saints,
and you, my brothers and sisters,
to pray for me to the Lord our
  God.
**(Sometimes we say another
prayer instead of this one.)**

PRIEST:
  May almighty God have mercy
    on us,
  forgive us our sins,
  and bring us to everlasting life.
PEOPLE: Amen.

PRIEST: Lord, have mercy.
PEOPLE: Lord, have mercy.

PRIEST: Christ, have mercy.
PEOPLE: Christ, have mercy.

PRIEST: Lord, have mercy.
PEOPLE: Lord, have mercy.

Glory to God in the highest,
and peace to his people on
earth.

Lord God, heavenly King,
almighty God and Father,
we worship you, we give you
thanks,
we praise you for your glory.

Lord Jesus Christ, only Son of
the Father,
Lord God, Lamb of God,
you take away the sin of the
world:
have mercy on us;
you are seated at the right
hand of the Father:
receive our prayer.

For you alone are the Holy One,
you alone are the Lord,
you alone are the Most High,
Jesus Christ,

with the Holy Spirit,
in the glory of God the Father.
Amen.

**WE STAND.**
**The priest prays for all our needs.**
**We answer: Amen.**

# LITURGY OF THE WORD

**We sit and listen with attention to the Word of God.**

**At the end of each reading the reader says,**

This is the Word of the Lord.

WE ANSWER: Thanks be to God.

**WE STAND.**

PRIEST: The Lord be with you.

PEOPLE: And also with you.

PRIEST: A reading from the holy gospel according to

_____.

PEOPLE: Glory to you, Lord.

**At the end of the Gospel the priest says,**

This is the Gospel of the Lord.

WE SAY: Praise to you, Lord Jesus Christ.

THE WORD OF GOD.

**The priest explains the Gospel to us.**

**WE STAND.**
**We recite the Creed to tell God that we believe everything he has taught us.**

We believe in one God,
    the Father, the Almighty,
    maker of heaven and earth,
    of all that is seen and unseen.

We believe in one Lord, Jesus
      Christ,
    the only Son of God,
    eternally begotten of the Father,
    God from God, Light from Light,
    true God from true God,
    begotten, not made, one in Being
      with the Father.
    Through him all things were
      made.

For us men and for our salvation
  he came down from heaven:

by the power of the Holy Spirit
  he was born of the Virgin Mary,
    and became man.

For our sake he was crucified
    under Pontius Pilate;
  he suffered, died, and was buried.

On the third day he rose again
    in fulfillment of the Scriptures;
  he ascended into heaven
    and is seated at the right hand
      of the Father.

He will come again in glory to judge
    the living and the dead,
  and his kingdom will have no
    end.

We believe in the Holy Spirit, the
    Lord, the giver of life,
  who proceeds from the Father and
    the Son.

With the Father and the Son he is
worshiped and glorified.
He has spoken through the
Prophets.
We believe in one holy catholic and
apostolic Church.
We acknowledge one baptism for
the forgiveness of sins.
We look for the resurrection of the
dead,
and the life of the world to come.
Amen.

**Next we pray for all the people
in the world.**

# LITURGY OF THE EUCHARIST

## Preparation of the Gifts

PRIEST:

Blessed are you, Lord, God of all creation.

Through your goodness we have this bread to offer,

which earth has given and human hands have made.

It will become for us the bread of life.

PEOPLE: Blessed be God for ever.

PRIEST:

Blessed are you, Lord, God of all creation.

Through your goodness we have this wine to offer,

PREPARATION OF THE GIFTS.

fruit of the vine and work of
human hands.
It will become our spiritual drink.
PEOPLE: Blessed be God for ever.

PRIEST: Pray...that our sacrifice may
be acceptable to God, the almighty
Father.
PEOPLE: May the Lord accept the
sacrifice at your hands
for the praise and glory of his
name,
for our good, and the good of all
his Church.

**WE STAND.**

PRIEST: The Lord be with you.
PEOPLE: And also with you.
PRIEST: Lift up your hearts.
PEOPLE: We lift them up to the Lord.
PRIEST: Let us give thanks to the
Lord our God.

PEOPLE: It is right to give him
    thanks and praise.


**The priest begins the most
important prayer of the Mass. It is
called the Eucharistic Prayer. At
the end of the first part of the
Eucharistic Prayer (the Preface)
we pray with the priest:**


PRIEST AND PEOPLE:
    Holy, holy, holy Lord, God
        of power and might,
    heaven and earth are full
        of your glory.
        Hosanna in the highest.
    Blessed is he who comes in the
        name of the Lord.
        Hosanna in the highest.

**WE KNEEL.**

The priest continues the Eucharistic Prayer. Then he comes to a very special point in the prayer. He holds the host (bread) and repeats the words of Jesus:

Take this, all of you, and eat it:
this is my body which will be
    given up for you.

**The bread has become the Body of Christ.**

**The priest raises the host for us to see.**

THE BREAD BECOMES THE
BODY OF CHRIST.

**Then the priest repeats the words of Jesus:**

Take this, all of you, and drink
    from it:
this is the cup of my blood,
the blood of the new and
    everlasting covenant.
It will be shed for you and for all,
so that sins may be forgiven.
Do this in memory of me.

**The wine has become the Blood of Christ.**

**The priest raises the chalice for us to see.**
**We adore Christ, present under the appearance of the bread and the wine.**

THE WINE BECOMES
THE BLOOD OF CHRIST.

PRIEST: Let us proclaim the mystery
   of faith:
PEOPLE: Christ has died,
      Christ is risen,
      Christ will come again.

**(Sometimes we use other words.)**

**In our hearts, we can pray:**

**Heavenly Father, your Son, Jesus Christ, died to make up for our sins. He also rose and went back to heaven with you. We offer you his Body and Blood for our salvation and for the salvation of all the people in the world.**

**At the end of the Eucharistic Prayer, the priest prays:**

PRIEST:
  Through him,
  with him,
  in him,
  in the unity of the Holy Spirit,
  all glory and honor is yours,
  almighty Father,
  for ever and ever.
PEOPLE: Amen.

## COMMUNION RITE

**WE STAND.**
PRIEST: Let us pray with confidence
  to the Father
  in the words our Savior gave us:

THE GREAT AMEN.

PEOPLE:

Our Father, who art in heaven,
hallowed be thy name;
thy kingdom come;
thy will be done on earth as it is
 in heaven.
Give us this day our daily bread;
and forgive us our trespasses
as we forgive those who trespass
 against us;
and lead us not into temptation,
but deliver us from evil.

PRIEST: Deliver us, Lord, from every
 evil,
and grant us peace in our day.
In your mercy keep us free from
 sin
and protect us from all anxiety
as we wait in joyful hope
for the coming of our Savior,
 Jesus Christ.

PEOPLE: For the kingdom, the power,

and the glory are yours, now and
   for ever.

PRIEST: The peace of the Lord be
   with you always.
PEOPLE: And also with you.

**We exchange a sign of peace
with the people who are near us.**

PEOPLE:
   Lamb of God, you take away the
         sins of the world:
      have hercy on us.

   Lamb of God, you take away the
         sins of the world:
      have mercy on us.

   Lamb of God, you take away the
         sins of the world:
      grant us peace.

COMMUNION.

PRIEST: This is the Lamb of God
who takes away the sins of the
world.
Happy are those who are called
to his supper.
PEOPLE: Lord, I am not worthy to
receive you,
but only say the word and I shall
be healed.

**We go up to receive the Lord Jesus in Holy Communion.**

**The priest says: "The Body of Christ."**
**We answer: "Amen," which means: we believe.**

**After Communion in our hearts we talk to our Friend, Jesus.**

# CONCLUDING RITE

**WE STAND.**

PRIEST: The Lord be with you.

PEOPLE: And also with you.

PRIEST:

    May almighty God bless you, the Father, and the Son, + and the Holy Spirit.

PEOPLE: Amen.

PRIEST:

    The Mass is ended, go in peace.

PEOPLE: Thanks be to God.

LAST BLESSING.

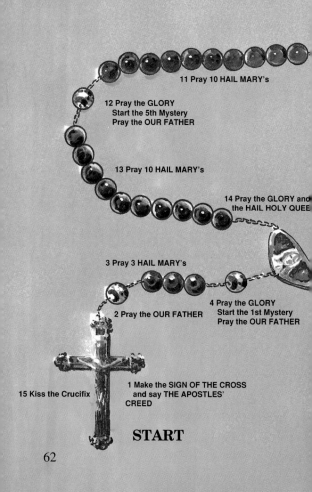

11 Pray 10 HAIL MARY's

12 Pray the GLORY
Start the 5th Mystery
Pray the OUR FATHER

13 Pray 10 HAIL MARY's

14 Pray the GLORY and
the HAIL HOLY QUEE

3 Pray 3 HAIL MARY's

2 Pray the OUR FATHER

4 Pray the GLORY
Start the 1st Mystery
Pray the OUR FATHER

15 Kiss the Crucifix

1 Make the SIGN OF THE CROSS
and say THE APOSTLES'
CREED

**START**

62

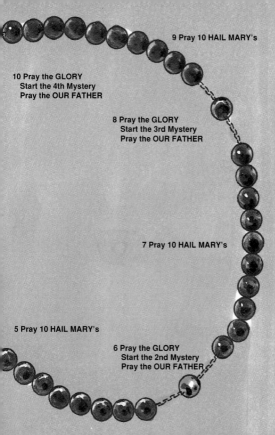

9 Pray 10 HAIL MARY's

10 Pray the GLORY
   Start the 4th Mystery
   Pray the OUR FATHER

8 Pray the GLORY
   Start the 3rd Mystery
   Pray the OUR FATHER

7 Pray 10 HAIL MARY's

5 Pray 10 HAIL MARY's

6 Pray the GLORY
   Start the 2nd Mystery
   Pray the OUR FATHER

# THE ROSARY

## THE JOYFUL MYSTERIES

Jesus, the Joyful Mysteries remind me of when you were a baby and a child. As I greet your Mother, I will think of how she watched and helped you to grow in wisdom and grace.

1. THE ANNUNCIATION OF THE
ARCHANGEL TO MARY.

2. THE VISITATION OF MARY TO
ST. ELIZABETH.

3. THE BIRTH OF JESUS IN THE STABLE
OF BETHLEHEM.

4. THE PRESENTATION OF JESUS
IN THE TEMPLE.

5. THE FINDING OF THE CHILD JESUS
IN THE TEMPLE.

## THE SORROWFUL
## MYSTERIES

Jesus, the Sorrowful Mysteries remind me of your passion and death. I will pray, thinking of how much you suffered to redeem us from sin. O Jesus, grant that I may willingly accept my own sufferings for your love.

1. Jesus prays in the garden of Gethsemane.

2. JESUS IS SCOURGED AT THE PILLAR.

3. Jesus is crowned with thorns.

4. Jesus carries the cross to Calvary.

5. The crucifixion and death
of Jesus.

## THE GLORIOUS MYSTERIES

Jesus, the Glorious Mysteries remind me of your victory over death and the gifts you gave your most holy Mother. As I pray, I will remember that if I stay close to you, I will be happy with you forever in heaven.

1. THE RESURRECTION OF JESUS.

2. THE ASCENSION OF JESUS
INTO HEAVEN.

3. THE HOLY SPIRIT DESCENDS UPON
THE APOSTLES.

4. THE ASSUMPTION OF THE
BLESSED VIRGIN MARY INTO HEAVEN.

5. THE CORONATION OF THE
BLESSED VIRGIN MARY.

# THE SACRAMENT OF RECONCILIATION

**In the Sacrament of Reconciliation the priest gives us the forgiveness of God and the Church.**

**There are five steps:**

1. *Think* of your sins.
2. *Be sorry* for your sins.
3. *Promise* Jesus that you will try not to sin again.
4. *Confess* (tell) your sins to the priest.
5. Do or pray the *penance* the priest gives you.

O Jesus, I am sorry.

# PRAYERS BEFORE
# AND AFTER
# RECONCILIATION

## PRAYER BEFORE
## RECONCILIATION

God my Father, you invite me closer to yourself through this sacrament. But some of my choices keep me from the happiness you want for me. Help me to remember: if I have said my prayers; if I go to Mass on Sunday; if I disobeyed; if I answered anyone back; if I said mean words; if I fought; if I stole; if I returned things I took.

Jesus, I am sorry for the times I did not follow your Way. I want to make better choices from now on.

Holy Spirit, fill me with trust as I celebrate the Sacrament of Reconciliation.

## PRAYER OF JOY AFTER RECONCILIATION

Jesus, you have forgiven me! Thank you for your pardon, dear Jesus. Show me how to be strong and loving.

God my Father, I promise to be a better child from now on.

Holy Spirit, help me to live and grow in your grace!

# COMMUNION PRAYERS

## BEFORE HOLY COMMUNION

Jesus, I believe that the Holy Eucharist is really you. Even though you are the Lord of heaven and earth, you come to visit me!

I am sorry for the times I have offended you. I promise that from now on I will try to be good, obedient and kind.

Help me grow in love for you and for everyone.

Mary, Mother of Jesus and my Mother, prepare my heart to receive your Son.

JESUS, I WANT TO RECEIVE YOU.

## AFTER HOLY COMMUNION

Dear Jesus, you have come into my heart.

Thank you, Jesus! May your kingdom come over the whole world. Bless our Pope, our Bishop and all your followers. Take care of all the people I love. Comfort people who are sick or lonely. Help all the people in the world to live in peace with you and with each other.

Mary, my heavenly Mother, help me to be always close to Jesus.

# THE STATIONS OF
# THE CROSS

**Kneel in front of the altar and say:**

Dear Jesus, who died to save me, I am here to remember your great love for me. I am sorry for the times I have not returned your love. May these Stations of the Cross open my heart more and more to your gifts of love!

**At each station, think of how Jesus suffered. Say the prayer of the station, then an "Our Father," a "Hail Mary," and a "Glory."**

# FIRST STATION

## Jesus Is Condemned to Death

"Christ suffered for you. He gave you an example to follow. So you should do as he did.

" 'He did no sin.

He never lied.' "

"People insulted Christ, but he did not insult them in return. Christ suffered, but he did not threaten. He let God take care of him" (1 Peter 2:21-23).

# SECOND STATION

## Jesus Takes Up His Cross

"Christ carried our sins in his body on the cross. He did this so that we would stop living for sin and start living for what is right. And we are healed because of his wounds" (1 Peter 2:24).

## THIRD STATION

### Jesus Falls the First Time

"If you are punished for doing wrong, there is no reason to praise you for bearing punishment. But if you suffer for doing good, and you are patient, then that pleases God" (1 Peter 2:20).

## FOURTH STATION

### Jesus Meets His Mother

"Simeon...said to Mary, '[Your son] will be a sign from God that many people will not accept....And the things that will happen will make your heart sad, too' " (Luke 2:34-35).

# FIFTH STATION

## Simon of Cyrene Helps Jesus

"Do not forget those who are in prison. Remember them as if you were in prison with them. Remember those who are suffering as if you were suffering with them" (Hebrews 13:3).

## SIXTH STATION

### Veronica Wipes Jesus' Face

" 'I was hungry, and you gave me food. I was thirsty, and you gave me something to drink. I was alone and away from home and you invited me into your house. I was without clothes, and you gave me something to wear. I was sick, and you cared for me. I was in prison, and you visited me.... Anything you did for any of my people here, you also did for me' " (Matthew 25:35-40).

## SEVENTH STATION

### Jesus Falls the Second Time

"If God is with us, then no one can defeat us. God let even his own Son suffer for us. God gave his Son for us all. So with Jesus, God will surely give us all things. Who can accuse the people that God has chosen? No one!" (Romans 8:31-33)

## EIGHTH STATION

## Jesus Meets the Good Women

"God chose you to be his people. I tell you now to live the way God's people should live. Always be humble and gentle. Be patient and accept each other with love" (Ephesians 4:1-2).

## NINTH STATION

### Jesus Falls the Third Time

"There are many things that Christ must still suffer through his body, the church. I am accepting my part of these things that must be suffered. I accept these sufferings in my body. I suffer for his body, the church" (Colossians 1:24).

# TENTH STATION

## Jesus' Clothes Are Torn Off

"Can anything separate us from the love Christ has for us? Can troubles or problems or sufferings? If we have no food or clothes, if we are in danger, or even if death comes—can any of these things separate us from Christ's love? I am sure nothing can separate us from the love God has for us" (Romans 8:35, 38).

# ELEVENTH STATION

## Jesus Is Nailed to the Cross

"Those who belong to Christ Jesus have crucified their own sinful selves. They have given up their old selfish feelings and the evil things they wanted to do. We get our new life from the Spirit. So we should follow the Spirit. We must not be proud. We must not make trouble with each other. And we must not be jealous of each other" (Galatians 5:24-26).

# TWELFTH STATION

## Jesus Dies on the Cross

"In your lives you must think and act like Christ Jesus.... He was equal with God. But he gave up his place with God and made himself nothing.

He was born to be a man
and became like a servant.

And when he was living as a man,

he humbled himself and was fully obedient to God.

He obeyed even when that caused his death—death on a cross.

So God raised Christ to the highest place. God made the name of Christ greater than every other name" (Philippians 2:5-9).

# THIRTEENTH STATION

## Jesus Is Taken from the Cross

"All I want is to know Christ and the power of his rising from death. I want to share in Christ's sufferings and become like him in his death. If I have those things, then I have hope that I myself will be raised from death" (Philippians 3:10-11).

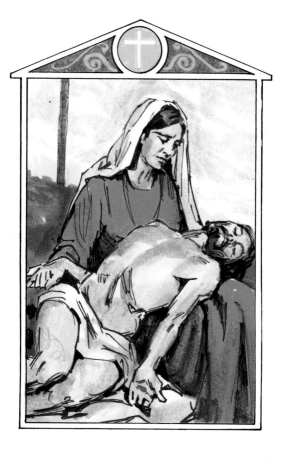

## FOURTEENTH STATION

### Jesus Is Laid in the Tomb

"We have sufferings now. But the sufferings we have now are nothing compared to the great glory that will be given to us. Everything that God made is waiting with excitement for the time when God will show the world who his children are" (Romans 8:18-19).

# FIFTEENTH STATION

## Jesus Rises from the Dead

"God raised the Lord Jesus from death. And we know that God will also raise us with Jesus. God will bring us together with you, and we will stand before him" (2 Corinthians 4:14).

O JESUS, I PROMISE
TO OBEY YOUR COMMANDMENTS.

Dear Jesus, help me always to remember your commandments. Grant that they may guide me in everything I do.

# THE TEN COMMANDMENTS

I am the Lord your God:

1. You shall not have strange gods before me.

I say my prayers every morning and night. I praise and adore God. This is how I keep God's first commandment.

2. You shall not take the Name of the Lord your God in vain.

I speak of God and of the saints and of holy things with respect and reverence. This is how I keep God's second commandment.

3. Remember to keep holy the Lord's day.

I join God's people at Mass on Sundays and holy days of obligation. I listen to God's Word. Together with the priest, I offer Jesus to the Father.

4. Honor your father and your mother.

I love and respect and obey my parents or guardians. I pay attention to my teacher in school. This is how I keep God's fourth commandment.

5. You shall not kill.

I take care of my body and soul. I never fight or quarrel or hurt anyone. I am kind to everybody. This is how I keep God's fifth commandment.

6. You shall not commit adultery.

I treat my body with respect. I watch only TV shows and videos that are good for children. This is how I keep God's sixth commandment.

7. You shall not steal.

I never take or damage what belongs to others. I am always honest and generous. This is how I keep God's seventh commandment.

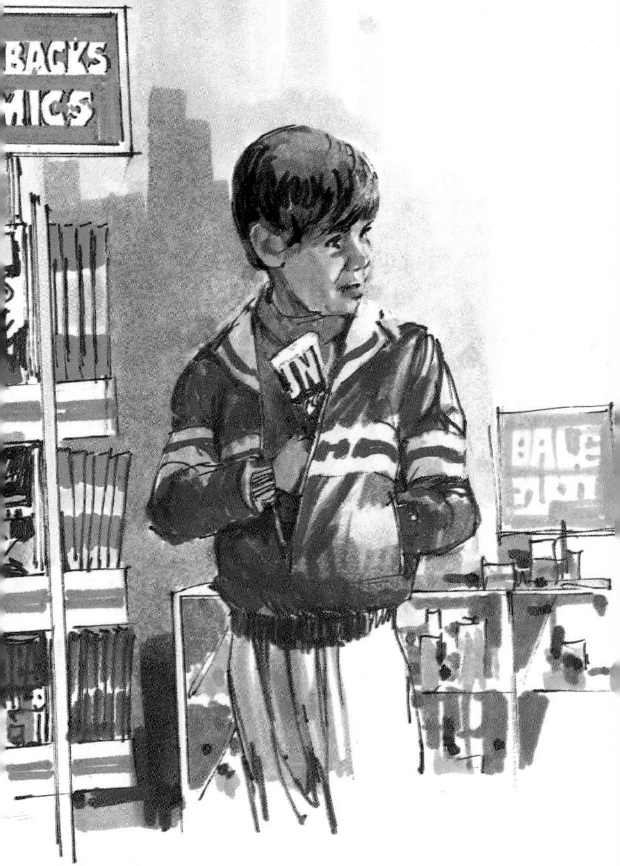
BACKS
MICS

8. You shall not bear false witness against your neighbor.

I never tell lies about anyone. I never speak of anyone's faults. I say only the truth. This is how I keep God's eighth commandment.

9. You shall not covet your neighbor's wife.

I remember that God gave each of us our bodies, and I am happy to respect my body and the bodies of others. This is how I keep God's ninth commandment.

10. You shall not covet your neighbor's goods.

I never want to take what belongs to others. I am never jealous. I am always satisfied. This is how I keep God's tenth commandment.

# THE SPECIAL DUTIES OF CATHOLICS

**Jesus, help me always to remember and live up to these special Duties of Catholic Christians:**

1. To worship God by participating in Mass every Sunday and holy day of obligation.

2. To receive Holy Communion often and the sacrament of Penance (Reconciliation) regularly.

3. To prepare for the sacrament of Confirmation by studying what our Catholic Church teaches us about this sacrament. To receive Confirmation, and then to always try to imitate Jesus, so that other

people can learn about Him from our example.

4. To obey the marriage laws of our Church.

5. To strengthen and support our Catholic Church by doing whatever we can to help out in our own parish, and by praying for our Holy Father the Pope, and for the Church all over the world.

6. To do penance for our sins, including giving up meat and fasting from food (when we are old enough to do this), on certain special days.

7. To pray for all missionaries who teach others about Jesus and to try to be missionaries ourselves, by imitating Jesus.

# THE SPIRITUAL
# WORKS OF MERCY

1. To admonish the sinner.

2. TO INSTRUCT THE IGNORANT.

3. To counsel the doubtful.

4. To comfort the sorrowful.

5. To bear wrongs patiently.

6. To forgive all injuries.

7. To pray for the living
and the dead.

# THE CORPORAL
# WORKS OF MERCY

1. To feed the hungry.

2. To GIVE DRINK TO THE THIRSTY.

3. To clothe the naked.

4. To visit the imprisoned.

5. To shelter the homeless.

6. To visit the sick.

7. To bury the dead.

# THE BEATITUDES

1. HAPPY THE POOR IN SPIRIT:
THEIRS IS THE KINGDOM OF HEAVEN.

2. HAPPY THOSE WHO MOURN:
THEY SHALL BE CONSOLED.

3. HAPPY THE HUMBLE:
THEY SHALL INHERIT THE LAND.

4. HAPPY THOSE WHO HUNGER AND
THIRST FOR HOLINESS:
THEY SHALL BE SATISFIED.

5. HAPPY THE MERCIFUL:
THEY SHALL FIND MERCY.

6. Happy the sincere of heart:
they shall see God.

7. Happy the peacemakers:
they shall be called
God's children.

8. Happy those who suffer
persecution for religion:
theirs is the kingdom of heaven.

# THE SEVEN SACRAMENTS

**Jesus, help me to live and grow in holiness through the sacraments —the powerful signs of your grace.**

1. Baptism.
2. Confirmation.
3. Holy Eucharist.
4. Penance (Reconciliation)
5. Anointing of the Sick.
6. Holy Orders.
7. Matrimony.

# BENEDICTION OF THE BLESSED SACRAMENT

## *O Saving Victim, Opening Wide*

O Saving Victim, opening wide
The gate of heav'n to us below!
Our foes press on from ev'ry side:
Thine aid supply, thy strength
  bestow.
To thy great name be endless
  praise,
Immortal Godhead, One in
  Three;
Oh, grant us endless length of
  days
In our true native land with thee.
Amen.

### *Humbly Let Us
Voice Our Homage*

Humbly let us voice our homage
For so great a sacrament:
Let all former rites surrender
To the Lord's New Testament;
What our senses fail to fathom
Let us grasp through faith's
  consent!
Glory, honor, adoration
Let us sing with one accord!
Praised be God, almighty Father;
Praised be Christ, his Son, our
  Lord;
Praised be God the Holy Spirit;
Triune Godhead be adored!
  Amen.

# THE DIVINE PRAISES

Blessed be God.

Blessed be his holy Name.

Blessed be Jesus Christ, true God
and true man.

Blessed be the Name of Jesus.

Blessed be his most Sacred
Heart.

Blessed be his most Precious
Blood.

Blessed be Jesus in the most holy
Sacrament of the altar.

Blessed be the Holy Spirit, the
Paraclete.

Blessed be the great Mother of
God, Mary most holy.

Blessed be her holy and immacu-
late conception.

Blessed be her glorious assumption.

Blessed be the name of Mary,
Virgin and Mother.
Blessed be St. Joseph, her most
chaste spouse.
Blessed be God in his angels and
in his saints.

# MY DEVOTIONS

## PRAYER TO THE
## SACRED HEART

Sacred Heart of my Jesus,
Keep me close to you;
Help me to love you always.
My Jesus, have mercy on me.
Jesus, meek and humble,
make my heart like yours.

SACRED HEART OF JESUS,
HAVE MERCY ON ME.

## PRAYER TO THE
## BLESSED MOTHER

Mary, Mother of Jesus and
    my Mother, too,
take care of me now and always.
Help me to love Jesus more and
    more,
Thank you, my sweet Mother.

MARY, MOTHER OF JESUS,
TAKE CARE OF ME NOW AND ALWAYS.

## PRAYER TO
## ST. DOMINIC SAVIO

Dear St. Dominic Savio,
you became holy doing your
    duties well.
Please make me obedient and
    holy too.
Obtain for me great love for
Jesus and Mary,
so that one day I may be
with them in heaven.

St. Dominic Savio, obtain for me
great love for Jesus and Mary.

## PRAYER TO
## ST. MARIA GORETTI

St. Maria Goretti,
because you loved Jesus so much
    you died rather than commit sin.
Help me to be courageous always
so that I may be pure and please
    Jesus, my God,
and share in your glory in
    heaven.

St. Maria Goretti, help me
to be pure and holy.

**ALASKA**
750 West 5th Ave., Anchorage, AK 99501 **907-272-8183.**
**CALIFORNIA**
3908 Sepulveda Blvd., Culver City, CA 90230 **213-397-8676.**
1570 Fifth Ave. (at Cedar Street), San Diego, CA 92101 **619-232-1442;**
**619-232-1443.**
46 Geary Street, San Francisco, CA 94108 **415-781-5180.**
**FLORIDA**
145 S.W. 107th Ave., Miami, FL 33174 **305-559-6715; 305-559-6716.**
**HAWAII**
1143 Bishop Street, Honolulu, HI 96813 **808-521-2731.**
**ILLINOIS**
172 North Michigan Ave., Chicago, IL 60601 **312-346-4228;**
**312-346-3240.**
**LOUISIANA**
4403 Veterans Memorial Blvd., Metairie, LA 70006 **504-887-7631;**
**504-887-0113.**
**MASSACHUSETTS**
50 St. Paul's Ave., Jamaica Plain, Boston, MA 02130 **617-522-8911.**
Rte. 1, 885 Providence Hwy., Dedham, MA 02026 **617-326-5385.**
**MISSOURI**
9804 Watson Rd., St. Louis, MO 63126 **314-965-3512; 314-965-3571.**
**NEW JERSEY**
561 U.S. Route 1, Wick Plaza, Edison, NJ 08817 **908-572-1200;**
**908-572-1201.**
**NEW YORK**
150 East 52nd Street, New York, NY 10022 **212-754-1110.**
78 Fort Place, Staten Island, NY 10301 **718-447-5071; 718-447-5086.**
**OHIO**
2105 Ontario Street (at Prospect Ave.), Cleveland, OH 44115
**216-621-9427.**
**PENNSYLVANIA**
214 W. DeKalb Pike, King of Prussia, PA 19406 **215-337-1882;**
**215-337-2077.**
**SOUTH CAROLINA**
243 King Street, Charleston, SC 29401 **803-577-0175.**
**TEXAS**
114 Main Plaza, San Antonio, TX 78205 **512-224-8101.**
**VIRGINIA**
1025 King Street, Alexandria, VA 22314 **703-549-3806.**
**CANADA**
3022 Dufferin Street, Toronto, Ontario, Canada M6B 3T5 **416-781-9131.**